T0303778

THE EREWASH VALLEY LINE

PAUL ROBERTSON

AMBERLEY

Front cover: No. 58025 passes Stanton Gate on the Up goods line with 7A12 07.30 Welbeck Colliery–Toton Yard, with an MGR bound for Ratcliffe Power Station. (2 October 1996)

Rear cover: Devon & Cornwall Railway's No. 56311 is seen passing Trowell Junction with 6Z57 14.45 Attercliffe–Chaddesden Yard scrap empties. (19 September 2012)

First published 2021

Amberley Publishing
The Hill, Stroud
Gloucestershire, GL5 4EP

www.amberley-books.com

Copyright © Paul Robertson, 2021

The right of Paul Robertson to be identified as the Author of this work has been asserted in accordance with the Copyrights, Designs and Patents Act 1988.

ISBN 978 1 3981 0396 2 (print)
ISBN 978 1 3981 0397 9 (ebook)

All rights reserved. No part of this book may be reprinted or reproduced or utilised in any form or by any electronic, mechanical or other means, now known or hereafter invented, including photocopying and recording, or in any information storage or retrieval system, without the permission in writing from the Publishers.

British Library Cataloguing in Publication Data.
A catalogue record for this book is available from the British Library.

Typesetting by SJmagic DESIGN SERVICES, India.
Printed in the UK.

Introduction

The origins of the Erewash Valley railway were borne out by the abundance of coal in the Nottinghamshire and Derbyshire coalfields, and the need for the coal owners to be able to transport their valuable product quickly to their main customers in industry and towns in Leicestershire. They would then be able to compete with the Leicester to Swannington railway, which commenced transporting coal from the Leicestershire coalfields in 1832. Plans were first drawn up in August 1832 to build the Erewash Valley Line to link Pinxton to a Long Eaton to Rugby line, but after much wrangling with rival railway companies and canal owners, the initial plans were scrapped. The first part of what we now call the Erewash Valley Line eventually opened as far as Codnor Park in 1847, with the first yard being established on the Toton site in 1856. The route was synonymous with the transportation of coal right through to the twenty-first century, but the sudden lurch away from fossil fuels for feeding our power stations over the last ten years has decimated the transport of coal by rail.

The Erewash Valley Line takes its name from the course of the River Erewash, which rises near Kirkby in Ashfield and follows the railway from Pye Bridge southwards through to Toton, weaving beneath the railway at eight locations, prior to passing under the Midland Main Line at Attenborough Junction and flowing into the River Trent. Although the river effectively only follows the railway for around half the length of the route, the whole railway corridor from Clay Cross through to the Trent Junction area is known as the Erewash Valley Line.

During early 1992, having gained promotion from the ticket office at Nottingham station to a position within the Inter-City Midland Cross Country control office based in Derby, house hunting began. This had to put me within public transport travelling distance of my new office, due to me not being able to drive at that time. A new home was found within walking distance of Attenborough station, and this also handily placed me around a mile and a half away from Toton yards and the Erewash Valley Line.

Around this time, with my change in job, I had a little more disposable income available, so I invested in more modern camera equipment, purchasing a Canon EOS 1000FN, replacing my Olympus OM10, also making the change from taking prints to colour slides. I didn't take driving lessons until later in the decade, so my main way of getting out and about with the camera was by push bike. I could often be found zipping along the towpath of the Erewash Canal between Trent, Toton and Stanton Gate to get me between locations. I occasionally ventured slightly further, but it wasn't until I joined the motoring masses that I visited locations further north on the Erewash regularly. Therefore, I am indebted to friends for lifts to get me around, and to the photographers who have kindly assisted me with providing their material to illustrate some of the locations where I have gaps on the Erewash.

When I moved to the area there was still an abundance of coal traffic on the Erewash, with many loading points still in use to feed the voracious appetites of the nearby Ratcliffe Power Station and the many others that were still active at the time. Prior to the introduction of the virtual quarry concept in 1998, there was also an abundance of ballast trains and trip workings that ran every weekday to the Leicestershire quarries at Mountsorrel, Croft, Bardon Hill and Stud Farm for loading wagons ready for weekend engineering works. The most famous of these ballast flows were the thrice-daily trains from Doncaster, which ran south to Mountsorrel, passing through Toton early morning, mid-morning and lunchtime, and back again northbound now loaded from late morning onwards. If I was off work or on a late shift and there was a hint of brightness, and with it being many years before the advent of 'gen' being freely available, I'd be phoning colleagues at work to find out what locos were working these trains, often basing my days photography around these workings – mainly Class 37 hauled, but 47s and 56s appeared fairly regularly.

The images reproduced in this book are aimed to give a visual walk through from south to north along and around the Erewash Valley Line, starting from Trent South Junction, stopping at the majority of vantage points and locations that spotters and photographers will have observed trains from over the years. Many of these locations have since been lost to either vegetation growth or redevelopment, and at several spots I have included more than one photo from different eras to show the 'then and now' changes of location, infrastructure, traffic flows and rolling stock types.

Due to space constraints, I can only briefly stop off at the Mecca that is Toton, but a follow up publication will concentrate on Toton depot and yards.

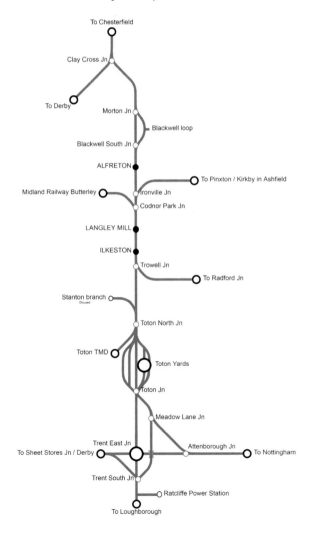

Brush Type 4 Class 47 No. 1806 is seen taking the Down high-level goods at Trent South Junction with the 15.30 Ratcliffe Power Station (seen looming in the background) to Toton Yard. Note the orange gas canisters, which were used for points heating and were left in situ all year round – we live in different times now and they wouldn't be there for long today. (16 July 1973; P. Robertson Collection)

At the same location, but looking north, No. 58021 *Hither Green Depot* approaches Trent South Junction with 6L60 17.31 Toton Yard–Temple Mills Yard departmental working. At the time Temple Mills was the hub for engineering trains in East Anglia, but upon its closure operations were transferred to March Whitemoor Yard. An engineers' trunk service still runs today at around the same time from Toton to Whitemoor, currently operated by GBRf. (4 June 1996)

No. 66789 *British Rail 1948–1997* has passed over Trent South Junction and is heading north on the Down high-level with 4E79 07.21 Ratcliffe PS–Doncaster Decoy Yard. This shot is taken from the road, which is below track level, with the use of a camera pole. (23 May 2019)

No. 37698 in the attractive orange and black Loadhaul livery, working in multiple with No. 37708 in Railfreight Petroleum livery, has just passed behind Trent PSB on the Up high-level goods with 7M63 08.19 Doncaster Wood Yard–Mountsorrel, which is conveying a high-output, ballast-cleaning train for reloading. The high-level lines link Toton to the Midland Main Line, crossing over the Trent to Nottingham line by an overbridge, thus reducing the number of conflicts at the busy Trent East Junction. (4 April 1997)

No. 37167, wearing Mainline Freight Aircraft Blue livery, comes off the Erewash Valley Line and is about to traverse Trent East Junction with 6T89 08.35 Toton Yard–Chaddesden sidings with ten Rudd wagons loaded with new ballast. These would be added to a weekend engineering train, which Chaddesden was still being used as a hub for at this time. (28 March 1997)

Romanian-built No. 56010 crosses Trent East Junction and takes the Down Erewash line with the 11.33 Denby DP–Ratcliffe PS MGR. Note the guards van, which the Denby services conveyed to allow staff to travel in to be able to disembark and operate the several manual crossings on the Denby branch. The following year this operation was replaced by a man in a van following the train. (17 February 1993)

We are now looking at the section between Trent East Junction and Toton South Junction, and in this wintry view No. 58014 *Didcot Power Station* is approaching the footbridge near north Erewash level crossing, Long Eaton, with 6A30 10.45 Toton Yard–Denby DP. As can be seen by the lack of brake vans on the train, the change to staff travelling by road to work the Denby line crossings has begun. (15 February 1994)

No. 60060 *James Watt* is seen at the same spot fourteen years later, with 6K50 15.12 Toton Yard–Crewe Basford Hall Yard infrastructure trip, which is conveying MRA side-tipping ballast wagons. The previous year the trees on the left had been cut down to ground level by Network Rail, but as can be seen they are already recovering well only one year on, and currently they are so large they prevent anything other than a head-on shot here. (13 October 2008)

The next footbridge north is at Long Eaton Town level crossing, which was the former footbridge at Long Eaton Town station. Looking south from the bridge, No. 37304 is passing the crossing box with a Derby St Mary's Yard–Toton Yard Speedlink trip. This box remained in use after the commissioning of Trent PSB in 1969, until closure came in October 1988 following the conversion of the crossing to CCTV operation controlled by the PSB. (10 May 1988; courtesy of C. Smith)

Passing beneath the former station footbridge and over the level crossing, No. 70007 passes Long Eaton Town with 4O95 12.12 Leeds FLT–Southampton MCT freightliner. The diversion of the freightliner traffic from the Derby route and on to the Erewash several years ago was a welcome addition to Erewash freight operations following the huge decline in coal traffic. (28 June 2019)

No. 67014 passes through the former station of Long Eaton Town with a very lightly loaded 6K50 15.12 Toton Yard–Crewe Basford Hall Yard on 31 July 2007. The brick wall visible was part of the platform infrastructure. The station failed to survive the Beeching review and officially closed on 2 January 1967.

No. 47323 is seen from a now removed footbridge at the north end of the former Long Eaton Town with 4L39 08.30 Washwood Heath Yard–Harwich PQ Yard with Rover cars for export. This train ran via Toton to run round, to reverse the wagons to be in the correct formation for unloading at Harwich. How many 1980s/early 1990s car types can you recognise in the car park? (18 August 1993)

This shot, which is taken from the car park in the previous picture, shows Virgin Cross Country's No. 47817 passing through with 1V64 12.17 Newcastle–Penzance, which was routed via the Erewash on Sundays at this time. (7 February 1999)

Eight years on and No. 37406 *The Saltaire Society* and Euro-Cargo Rail-branded No. 66246 pass Long Eaton Town with 6G45 16.38 Toton Yard–Bescot Yard infrastructure working. (1 May 2007)

Viewed from the Nottingham Road overbridge in Long Eaton, No. 56099 is nearing journey's end with 6G25 04.11 Bescot Yard–Toton Yard with four Salmon wagons loaded with concrete sleepers. (13 June 1998)

No. 66117 is seen from the same vantage point twenty years later, with 6B09 07.12 Derby North Junction–Toton Yard returning from the Derby remodelling blockade. Changes of note are the removal of the footbridge at Long Eaton Town and the Tesco superstore now providing the backdrop, with only the tip of the power station chimney remaining visible. (3 June 2018)

Looking north towards Toton from Nottingham road bridge, No. 47323 has run round in Toton to reverse the consist of 4L39 08.30 Washwood Heath Yard–Parkeston Quay Yard with another load of Rover cars for export. No. 31106 is waiting to head north with 6E71 Bescot Yard–Healey Mills Yard infrastructure trip. (19 November 1993)

Fast forward almost twenty-seven years and No. 37423 *Spirit of the Lakes* has just passed through Toton with 6Z37 12.06 Shirebrook W. H. Davis–Crewe Basford Hall Yard conveying eight new FNA flats and cases for transporting nuclear waste. (14 March 2019)

Another shot from this location, this time showing the new company livery for Freightliner (parent company Genesee and Wyoming's colours) on No. 66413 *Lest We Forget,* with 4O95 12.12 Leeds FLT–Southampton MCT, which is being held to time as the train often does here after running early from Chesterfield up the Erewash Valley. (25 April 2019)

A step closer to Toton, No. 47336 is seen departing with a loaded MGR, passing beneath the flyover that linked the high-level goods lines at Toton East Junction to the North Yard and Down-side hump. (13 October 1980; P. Robertson Collection)

No. 37016 is seen at the same spot as it arrives light engine en route to Toton TMD, and not a lot seems to have changed in the intervening three years. (5 July 1983; P. Robertson Collection)

However, jumping forward again, this time by a massive thirty-three years, sees Freightliner's No. 66516 slowing for its usual pathing stop with 4O95 12.12 Leeds FLT–Southampton MCT. The passage of time has seen the vegetation take over, the high-level bridge taken out of use, and the area resignalled. (17 March 2016)

Looking back south towards Long Eaton Town, Nos 20182 and 20159 approach Toton with a trip with repaired wagons from the BR wagon repair shops at Wetmore, Burton upon Trent. Prominent in the frame are the town's former gasometer and the semaphore signal, which protected the oil terminal when the ground frame was reversed for trains to arrive and depart. (21 July 1986; courtesy of C. Smith)

Sixteen years on and the gasometer has gone, and a communications mast stands in its place. The signal, however, lives on, even though the line into the oil terminal it once protected has long since been removed. Loadhaul-liveried No. 37710 passes with 6T21 16.03 Chaddesden Sidings–Toton Yard spoil empties. (16 May 2002)

Viewed from the redundant flyover bridge, which was out of use by the mid-1980s, No. 58009 approaches Toton with MGR empties, likely to be from Ratcliffe PS. The wasteland to the right would see redevelopment with an Asda built close to the road bridge, and the land closer to the camera in industrial use. (14 April 1988; P. Robertson Collection)

The backdrop and right foreground have changed in the eight years between this and the picture of No. 58009. Here No. 37718 approaches Toton with 6Z43 08.30 from Tavistock Junction, which is an empty pipe train returning to Toton after delivering its load from Stanton. (25 October 1996)

Moving across to the high-level lines, here No. 37503 is working hard on the climb up to the site of the former Toton East Junction with 6M63 08.19 Doncaster Wood Yard–Mountsorrel. My vantage point here was the embankment of the lifted flyover line, which had brambles but trees had not yet taken hold. (14 January 1997)

Viewed from the opposite side of the line is No. 37071 taking the Up high level with 7M64 05.58 Doncaster Wood Yard–Mountsorrel conveying a Redland self-discharge set. These trains, running up to three trips per day, were the mainstay of my local photography at the time, but the invention of the 'virtual quarry' concept was soon to be their death knell. (22 June 1998)

Nos 20187 and 20052 thunder over Toton Junction and are starting to tackle the incline up to Meadow Lane Junction with another load of coal for Ratcliffe PS. Even in midsummer the MGR trains would keep topping up the stockpiles ready for winter. (30 August 1990; courtesy of C. Smith)

Six years on and not a lot has changed. No. 58002 *Daw Mill Colliery* takes the high-level with the 7A15 13.32 Doe Hill–Ratcliffe PS MGR. The loco was still adorned with stickers from a railtour that it worked from Retford to Aberdeen and back with No. 58046 the previous month. This view is now lost to trees. (23 October 1996)

No. 60090 *Quinag* is seen in Long Eaton oil terminal putting together the empties to form the 6E50 15.55 to Port Clarence. The terminal didn't have too long left in operation at this time, and soon after its closure it partly disappeared beneath a new Asda overflow car park during rebuilding and relocation of the original store, although some of the trackbed and rails are still evident near to the flyover bridge. (3 August 1993)

No. 56087 is seen from the footbridge as it shunts to split its train into the discharge sidings at Long Eaton oil terminal with a train from Port Clarence. (29 April 1993; courtesy of C. Smith)

Fresh out of the box, No. 58027 passes over Toton Junction with an MGR for Ratcliffe Power Station on 24 April 1985. There has been so much change since this view: housing development, loss of infrastructure, traction and wagon changes, plus a lot of vegetation growth. (Courtesy of C. Smith)

Amazingly, I was the only person on the bridge to witness Nos 37427 and 37411 *Ty Hafan* depart from Toton with the 1Z46 15.20 Toton TMD–Kings Cross special. It was believed to be transporting dignitaries that had received a tour of the EWS facility, possibly connected to the forthcoming Class 66 investment. (13 October 1997)

The footbridge over the main lines at Toton was known locally as 'Long Tom' and a smaller bridge over the departure lines from the East Yard was 'Little Tom'. Here No. 25276 departs with a mixed bag of wagons approaching Long Tom bridge at 16.10 on 25 August 1985. (P. Robertson Collection)

Class 20s worked great together in pairs, but I always liked seeing single 20s working trains. Here, No. 20170 and a brake van are arriving back at Toton from the south on a misty 25 September 1985. (P. Robertson Collection)

No. 40079 is seen descending the high-level goods line from Toton East Junction with a train of scrap from Corby or Snailwell heading for either Stanton or Aldwarke. (8 October 1984; courtesy of C. Smith)

Twelve years on and No. 37719 descends to Toton Junction with 6E77 14.32 Mountsorrel–Doncaster Wood Yard loaded ballast. Lots of change has occurred. (16 July 1996)

Ex-works-condition No. 56117 passes Toton Junction with 7M64 05.58 Doncaster Wood Yard–Mountsorrel empty ballast. Disused railway buildings on view – and soon to be removed – include the Down hump control tower and Toton Centre signal box. (2 September 1997)

It's like *Wacky Races* to see who can get to Ratcliffe PS first on 19 August 2013. The attractive powder-blue-liveried No. 60074 *Teenage Spirit* is lumbering out of North Yard with 6M22 22.48 Liverpool BT–Ratcliffe PS, as No. 66549 races by with another imported coal from Immingham HIT to Ratcliffe PS. Southbound departures from the Down side were made possible with the completion of the Erewash south resignalling works.

No. 47315 is approaching Toton on the Down main line with 6E79 17.01 Mountsorrel–Doncaster Wood Yard on a warm and sunny 4 June 1997.

This footbridge was a regular haunt for me to view the 'Chadd trip', which conveyed spoil for unloading at the tip, and occasionally empty wagons or loaded ballast for forming into engineering trains ready for weekend works. On 9 May 1997, No. 31465, in Regional Railways livery, departs with 6T89 08.10 Toton Old Bank–Chaddesden Yard.

No. 37426 comes down the high-level and sweeps over Toton Junction on Sunday 25 May 2003 with 7B04 15.00 Bedford–Toton Old Bank Yard conveying a long train of ZBA Rudd wagons loaded with spoil from an engineering renewals site.

No. 56090 approaches Toton on the Down goods with 6E97 15.55 Corby–Aldwarke conveying loaded scrap in SSA wagons. The second man appears to be filming the trip and new palisade steel fencing now lines the railway boundary. (12 April 2003)

Moving up to Toton 'bank' we see No. 58044 *Oxcroft Opencast* waiting to depart New Bank Yard with 7A15 08.47 to Ratcliffe PS, and No 58014 *Didcot Power Station* is backing down on to the 08.35 to Nadins DP. As is the case with Class 60s today, this yard was used for the storage of withdrawn Class 31s, and prominent at the head of the line are Nos 31290, 31294 and 31116. (14 August 1997)

Five years later and change is in the air. New Bank Yard has seen investment, with the south end connections to the nearest five roads reconnected, EWS livery, and Class 66s and HTA wagons have appeared and are making inroads into the old order. No. 60022, on overhauled bogies, departs from New Bank with another train of coal for Ratcliffe PS. (24 August 2002)

I always felt like a kid in a sweetshop on visits to Toton depot, especially when the sun was shining. On one such visit, seen awaiting their turns for attention, are Nos 58010, 37047 and 37719. Stored No. 37073 can also be glimpsed in the north headshunt in the distance. (29 May 1999)

An overview of the north end of Toton TMD taken from the A52 bridge on 31 May 2009. On view are forty-two Class 60s, nine Class 66s, four Class 08s and two withdrawn Class 58s. The proximity of Ratcliffe Power Station can also be seen in this view.

If anyone invents the means to time travel, would this be the era to return to? Class 20s No. 8136 and green-liveried No. 8016 depart from Toton with a mixed, loaded train of mineral wagons. A mostly empty shed front suggests there was plenty of work at this time. (10 May 1973; P. Robertson Collection)

What a contrast this is to the May 1973 picture. No. 66140 is departing Toton with 4H04 17.33 to Peak Forest on Sunday 23 April 2017. New Bank is littered with stored wagons and Class 60 locos. The depot also has an abundance of idle Type 5 power and only ghosts of unfitted freight trains remain.

In wonderful lighting, No. 58016 arrives at Toton with 7A23 18.04 Daw Mill–Ratcliffe PS MGR. The train will back into New Bank Yard and run round prior to heading to Ratcliffe to unload. (10 June 1998)

In midsummer it's just possible to get early morning light scraping on the front of northbound trains, and a curved front of a Class 37 certainly helped. Here, Loadhaul-liveried No. 37517 arrives at Toton with 6G25 05.03 Bescot ES–Toton Yard. Can you spot a Class 20 and a 142 unit on shed? (26 July 2003)

A view of Stapleford and Sandiacre ballast sidings from the A52 bridge sees yard pilot No. 60054 *Charles Babbage* engaged in shunting loaded Seacow wagons. This was taken on the way home from a night shift, and after taking this shot I returned to the car for a lens change and promptly locked my keys in the boot, which delayed my sleep even longer! (2 June 2009)

Looking north from the A52 bridge, No. 60042 passes Stapleford and Sandiacre shunt frame box with 6Z82 05.17 Port Clarence–Kingsbury loaded oil tanks. The railway location took both names of the locality as the railway is the divide between the two towns. (6 August 1997)

Fast forward twenty-two years later and No. 37057 is pushing 1Q64 08.52 Derby RTC–Doncaster West Yard PLPR test train. Spot the differences. (23 September 2019)

Viewed from Derby road bridge, No. 58032 arrives at Stapleford and Sandiacre with a set of MGR empties from Ratcliffe PS. The train will stop clear of the 'ground' position signal, then set back into New Bank Yard. This was also the site of the former station of the same name, closed by Beeching in 1967. (8 July 1986; courtesy of C. Smith)

Nos 37055 and 37683 power away from Toton with 7E27 14.56 Bardon Hill–Doncaster Decoy Yard conveying boulders for sea defence works in the Hull area. (7 June 1999)

No. 56075 *West Yorkshire Enterprise* passes Stapleford on the approach to Toton with a loaded MGR. The lineside factory was the Old Cross Dye Works, now long gone – they don't design factories like that anymore. (27 May 1986; J. S. Mattison/P. Robertson Collection)

By 2010 the scene is much changed, with the dye works gone, Stanton pipe works missing from the horizon and the large trees also removed. The area has been remodelled and resignalled, with signalling now controlled from the EMCC at Derby. No. 60074 *Teenage Spirit* and No. 66132 are arriving at Toton with 6H90 13.00 Thoresby Colliery Junction–Toton Yard with a HOBC set from the Network Rail High Marnham test track. (17 April 2010)

No. 60019 *Port of Grimsby and Immingham* passes Stapleford with the diverted 6M57 05.48 Lindsey OR–Kingsbury oil tanks during the closure of Nottingham station for remodelling and resignalling. (14 August 2013)

Seen from the footbridge just north of Stapleford & Sandiacre is No. 40057, which is almost at its destination with the 12.46 Ashburys–Toton Speedlink. The outward morning trip from Toton emanated from the east yard and ran via Beeston, Lenton and Radford junctions to reach the Erewash at Trowell Junction to head north. (14 June 1984; courtesy of C. Smith)

One of the most colourful workings on the Erewash Valley Line were the overhauled 1973 tube stock movements. Here, No. 37013 passes Stapleford with 8X10 09.25 Horbury Prorail–Didcot Yard running five hours late. Not driving at that time, I raced off in pursuit on my pushbike and was rewarded with another shot of the train leaving Toton after the loco had been swapped for No. 37244. (7 August 1996)

An unusual but welcome choice for a wagon transfer from Toton to Worksop, No. 37513 heads north at Stapleford with MGR empties. (3 June 1997)

Following the culling of the giant poplar trees, a northbound shot was made possible from the footbridge, illustrated here by No. 66531 passing with 6M90 02.57 West Thurrock–Earles Sidings empty cement. (16 June 2010)

No. 58048, with the original EW&S branding, sweeps south through Stapleford with 6K94 14.05 Worksop Yard–Toton Yard MGR transfer. The view here was blighted by the installation of a large signal gantry during the Erewash resignalling project. (9 June 1997)

Heading north towards Stanton Gate, the canal towpath borders the railway and here affords a view of Mainline Blue-liveried No. 60011 heading 7A17 12.40 Bilsthorpe Colliery–Ratcliffe PS along the Up goods line. (9 April 1996)

From the opposite side of the line, where Stanton Gate sidings once existed, No. 37515 is seen passing St Giles' Church at Sandiacre with 7M63 08.19 Doncaster Wood Yard–Mountsorrel empty ballast conveying vacuum braked Tope wagons. (15 May 1997)

Onto the footbridge at Stanton Gate and No. 37059 is seen in immaculate condition heading along the Up goods with 1Q14 09.36 Derby RTC–Derby RTC, which visited many East Midlands routes on two consecutive sunny days with a radio survey test train. No. 37609 is on the rear of the train. This view of the Up goods (now known as the Up Erewash Slow), like many others, became overgrown and was lost to vegetation growth; however, some work early in 2020 has made this view at least temporarily possible again.

The view at Stanton Gate on the sweeping curve is a classic, and is still possible today, albeit with a backdrop of trees rather than the canal. Nos 20026 and 20136 pass a row of withdrawn classmates with a Bentinck Colliery to Ratcliffe PS MGR. (16 March 1990; courtesy of C. Smith)

In my opinion Class 60s looked very smart in Loadhaul colours, illustrated by No. 60059 *Swinden Dalesman* passing Stanton Gate with 6Z90 04.53 Lackenby Yard–Corby steelworks with hot rolled-steel coils. This was a second additional path to move coils to Corby, which ran as required. Corby steelworks is still in production and is now served by a daily train from Margam Yard with steel coil from Port Talbot works. (17 September 1997)

No. 56096 passes the site of the closed Stanton Gate Up Yard, with the first signs of nature starting to reclaim the land. (23 July 1984; courtesy of C. Smith)

By 2013, nature has done pretty well. No. 66719 *METRO-LAND* passes Stanton Gate with 6V09 14.32 Tunstead–Brentford loaded stone. Silver birch trees seem to thrive on former railway formations. (19 August 2013)

No. 37884 *Gartcosh* passes beneath Stanton Gate footbridge with 7M63 08.19 Doncaster Wood Yard–Mountsorrel, conveying Seacow ballast hoppers for loading at the quarry. (21 April 1997)

No. 47826 *Springburn* heads north through Stanton Gate with 1Z33 06.38 Bedford–Carlisle West Coast Railways charter. This was the first photography outing with my now eldest daughter in tow; amazingly, it had taken eight months for her first photography trip to occur. (10 June 2006)

The unusual sight and sound of a Class 33 Crompton on the Erewash Valley Line as No. 33021 *Eastleigh* pilots 4MT 2-6-4T No. 80098 and its support coach, running as 5Z95 22.12 Hither Green–Butterley Midland Railway Centre. (1 September 1999)

At Moorbridge Lane bridge, Stanton Gate, No. 60071 *Ribblehead Viaduct* passes the former station site with 6M73 10.55 Doncaster Down Decoy Yard–Toton Yard. The Mapperley branch, latterly serving Stanton pipe works, which diverges to the left, was mothballed after the closure of Stanton pipe works in 2007, but brought back into use during early 2021. (1 March 2010)

Passing Stanton Gate on the Down goods line, No. 37264 pilots No. 37109 on 6M21 09.11 Toton Yard–Castleton, which was a daily train for collecting new CWR for renewing the rails on the national network. Due to its out and back nature, Toton used the train regularly for testing locos after attention or overhaul. Note No. 37109 has been overhauled but only the roof has so far been painted with primer. No. 47331 is passing on the Up main, engaged in route learning duties. (20 August 1996)

Nos 20136 and 20105 wait to depart from Ward's of Ilkeston with a scrap metal train for Cardiff Tidal Yard. This siding was located from a spur from the Stanton Gate to Mapperley branch line, and the Wards scrap yard still exists here. In the Spring of 2021 Wards have recommenced sending scrap out by train, albeit moved the short distance by road to the former Stanton pipe site for loading. (19 March 1986; courtesy of D. Peachey)

In summer 1997 the Stanton Ironworks Company commenced a contract with EWS to transport pipes by rail to Immingham for export by sea to Peru. The stub of the Mapperley branch, which was extant up to approximately a half mile from the pipe works was used – this was often used to stable the royal train overnight when the monarchy were visiting the East Midlands. The pipes were brought to the train by lorry, with a crane loading them onto the wagons. A mix of Toton Yard pilots and main line locos were used, and here No. 08441 is seen awaiting the completion of loading of the first train of the contract. (16 July 1997)

The line was later extended into the works, with a loop installed to allow the empty trains from Toton to run round and then propel into the works loading area. Here No. 56100 is standing in the loop at Stanton waiting to depart with 6E67 07.08 to Tees Dock. (28 July 2003)

No. 58047 is seen departing from the pipe works confines at Stanton, among the piles of scrap, with 8T01 11:30 to Toton Yard on 4 March 2000. Many years previously scrap was brought into Stanton, and there was talk around this time of loaded scrap trains resuming as well as trains bringing the other raw materials required in the cast-iron-making industry. However, this was not to be, and the pipe production plant eventually closed in May 2007. In spring 2021 rail operations have resumed to the Mapperley branch with scrap trains for Wards recycling, and there are also plans for aggregates and container loading terminals to be built.

In previous years the Mapperley branch served two coal-loading disposal points – at Mapperley and West Hallam. Seen at Stanton Gate, with the last train from West Hallam, is No. 58014, which is also bringing No. 08814 back to Toton after it had been on hire to Hargreaves for use at the disposal point. (11 October 1985; courtesy of D. Peachey)

No. 08441 is seen again, with the first train of the Peru contract, coming off the Mapperley branch at Stanton Gate. Prior to departure the crew have obviously found a vehicle registration plate in the undergrowth, which now adorns the front of the shunt loco. (16 July 1997)

Laying down a trail of exhaust with full power applied, No. 37798 is seen from the embankment of the M1 overbridge as it passes Stanton Gate with 6M21 09.11 Toton Yard–Castleton empty CWR train. (24 September 1996)

Seen from the north side of the M1 bridge at Stanton Gate, West Coast Railway's No. 57601 is top and tailing with No. 57001 as it heads south with 1Z57 06.10 Sheffield–Llandudno charter. (2 May 2011)

Moving north again to the footbridge just south of Trowell Junction, No. 31454 *The Heart of Wessex* is seen powering 6Z59 12.02 Shirebrook W. H. Davis–Derby, consisting of timber wagons converted from former cargo waggons. At Derby, Virgin Trains' No. 57310, which had been hired by Colas Rail, took the train forward to Carlisle for use on their timber flow to Chirk. (4 April 2007)

I had a massive slice of luck with this one. While out at Trowell for a test train, info came through about No. 56098 being with No. 66727 on 4Z27 12.55 Hotchley Hill–Middlesbrough empty gypsum to get the Class 56 to Doncaster for tyre turning, prior to heading back to shunt duties at Peak Forest. I thought the loco would be tucked inside the Class 66, but luck was on my side and the loco turned up on the front of the train, with the 66 on the rear. (4 July 2019)

No. 37513 heads south from Trowell Junction with 6M63 08.19 Doncaster Wood Yard–Mountsorrel ballast. Prior to the virtual quarry concept, it was common to see trains such as this with only part of the train requiring loading. The best I ever saw was a full train of Seacow wagons, with only one requiring refilling. (19 August 1996)

One of the earliest Class 60s to be withdrawn, No. 60098 *Charles Francis Brush* passes Trowell with 6P27 07.45 Rufford–Toton Yard empty coal, with Rufford having received the loaded train with coal for blending. (19 August 1996)

A couple of shots just onto the Trowell branch now. This route lets Nottingham-bound traffic avoid Toton, running direct from Trowell Junction to Radford Junction. Here No. 47439 is just approaching the junction at Trowell with 1M12 13.20 Harwich PQ–Blackpool North. St Helen's Church in Trowell village helps to frame the shot. (26 May 1986; courtesy of C. Smith)

No. 37419 *Carl Haviland* top and tailing with No. 37402 *Stephen Middlemore 23.12.1954-8.6.2013* have just taken the branch at Trowell Junction working 1Q50 13.40 Derby RTC–Cleethorpes–Doncaster West Yard PLPR test train. Taken with a camera pole. (6 June 2019)

Due to the derailment of an MGR coal train on 1 September 1988, which pretty much demolished the point work on the main lines at Trowell, the junction was removed and plain lined until new points were manufactured and ready to be installed. The new points are seen in the Down cess five days before installation as Nos 20176 and 20145 pass on an engineers working. (20 March 1990; courtesy of D. Peachey)

No. 37379 *Ipswich WRD Quality Assured* blasts away from a signal check and crosses Trowell Junction with 8X09 20.12 Didcot Yard–Horbury Prorail with 1973 tube stock for overhaul. (16 August 2000)

Looking north from the road bridge at Trowell, No. 43048 *T.C.B. Miller MBE* crosses the junction to gain the Up Trowell line to Radford Junction with the 13.05 Sheffield–Nottingham ECS on a snowy 11 February 2012.

On a much warmer day, Colas Rail-operated No. 66848 heads south over Trowell Junction working 6M86 10.45 Wolsingham–Ratcliffe PS coal. (11 July 2013)

Seen from the footbridge, in ex-works condition, No. 37667 heads north through Trowell Junction on 8E78 14.30 Mountsorrel–Doncaster Decoy Yard. Note the abutments attached to the road bridge, which supported the station building and stairs to the former station platforms. (15 May 1997)

On a day of showers and not much in the way of sunshine, luck was eventually on my side, providing some nice winter light on Europhoenix-liveried No. 37608 as it hauled Crossrail unit No. 345023 through Trowell Junction as 5Q58 14.58 Worksop Yard–Old Dalby. The storage of new trains at Worksop, pending their acceptance, has provided welcome new workings along the Erewash, mostly operated with heritage traction. (17 February 2020)

No. 58011 *Worksop Depot* approaches Trowell Junction with 7G44 13.00 Oxcroft–Toton Yard for later forwarding to Rugeley PS. The lift gear of the now defunct dry ski slope at Cossall can be seen atop the hill in the distance. (15 May 1997)

The lattice footbridge at Trowell Junction is mooted to be up for renewal. Here, No. 66706 *Nene Valley* pulls away from a signal check and passes beneath the bridge with 6Z40 05.00 Wellingborough Yard–Tunstead. (15 July 2013)

Furnace Road, which parallels the railway from Trowell Junction, provides fond memories for me. With my father working in nearby Ilkeston, he would often take me and park up here to watch the passing trains. Glinting in the low winter sun, No. 20210, plus a brake van, heads by during one such visit. (18 February 1987)

Freightliner-operated No. 66623, in the new house colours of holding company Genesee & Wyoming, approaches Trowell Junction with 6Z37 11.48 Tunstead–Elstow stone in lucky light, taken with the camera mounted on a pole. (2 December 2019)

Taken from the footbridge at Potters Lock, Cossall, Nos 20055 and 20005 power north on the Down goods line with empty HTV wagons. (8 July 1985; courtesy of B. Dean)

The original lattice footbridge having now been replaced by an ugly modern version, No. 43102 *The Journey Shrinker 148.5 MPH The Worlds Fastest Diesel Train*, repainted by EMR to celebrate the end of HST operation with the company, leads 1B23 06.34 Leeds–St Pancras, with No. 43295 on the rear. (12 April 2021)

No. 45066 heads south along the Up main at Cossall, near Ilkeston, with the 10.00 Beighton Yard–Loughborough Yard empty ballast. It has just passed No. 31415 on a Harwich PQ–Blackpool North service. Having been dropped off by my father on his way to work in Ilkeston, I spent the day here between approximately 8.00 and 16.00 and my spotting notes show I observed forty-five locomotive-hauled trains – oh for a time machine. (14 April 1987)

No. 56087 heads north along the Down goods line at Ilkeston with MGR empties. The background is dominated by the large Armstrongs Mill, which is now in retail use. (17 June 1986; J. S. Mattison/PR Collection)

Work is underway on the foundations for the rebirth of Ilkeston station on the site of the original Ilkeston Junction & Cossall station, which was closed like many others on the Erewash on 2 January 1967. Inter-City-liveried No. 37254 is seen pushing a PLPR test train north along the Down Erewash fast line. (29 August 2016; courtesy of V. Hardy)

No. 66606 passes through the completed Ilkeston station with 6M73 10.50 Doncaster Decoy Yard–Toton Yard infrastructure service on 30 December 2019. The station was opened on Sunday 2 April 2017 and is mostly served by an hourly Northern Rail service between Nottingham and Leeds, with a handful of EMR services also calling here.

In 2008 a bypass was constructed between Ilkeston and Awsworth, crossing the Erewash just north of the station site. Here No. 70004 is seen from the bridge with 6L89 12.37 Earles Sidings–West Thurrock cement. (15 April 2014)

The next road bridge to the north affords excellent views of the former GNR viaduct at Bennerley. No. 58022 is seen running along the Up goods line with 7G41 09.21 Thoresby Colliery–Rugeley PS – the Down goods was now out of use following a derailment. In the Erewash resignalling of 2008, both goods lines were replaced by a single Up and Down bidirectional slow line. (9 October 1998)

Twenty years on and nature has reclaimed the disused disposal point siding. No. 56096 heads south with 6C70 07.40 Dore Station Junction–Toton Yard engineering train. (Sunday 20 May 2018)

Bennerley Disposal Point received a short-term flow in early 1993, with coal brought in from Blindwells in Scotland for blending prior to being reloaded into MGR wagons and taken to Ratcliffe PS. Here, No. 56010 has unloaded and will shortly propel back to then exit south as 6Z53 15.25 to Millerhill Yard via a run round in Toton Yard. (15 March 1993; courtesy of D. Peachey)

Seen from atop Bennerley Viaduct is ex-works No. 58039 *Rugeley Power Station*, in unbranded Railfreight triple-grey, heading north with 6E19 11.12 Mountfield–Milford gypsum empties. The now closed dry ski slope at Cossall is evident and the hill on which it stood is a former colliery tip and is now classed as a nature reserve. (18 July 1994; courtesy of D. Peachey)

No. 66529 heads north at Bennerley with 4E77 07.30 Ratcliffe PS–Barrow Hill sidings empty coal. The origin location of the train is visible on the skyline. (8 June 2015)

Nos 20096 and 20107 top and tail with Nos 20132 and 20118 *Saltburn-By-The-Sea* at Bennerley working 6M20 06.49 Barrow Hill depot–Old Dalby, en route to take an LUL S-Stock set to Amersham. The viaduct can be accessed from the canal towpath, and the eventual plan is for it to carry a footpath and cycle route between Ilkeston and Awsworth. This great work is being carried out by the Friends of Bennerley Viaduct group. (26 May 2014)

Within Bennerley D. P. No. 58009 arrives with a set of MGR empties from Toton. The disposal point was getting close to closure at this time. (26 April 1994; courtesy of D. Peachey)

Seen from close to the canal towpath just north of the viaduct, No. 60020 *The Willows* passes Bennerley with 6E08 15.02 Wolverhampton Steel terminal–Immingham. Taken with the camera mounted on a pole. (10 August 2018; courtesy of V. Hardy)

Our next vantage point is the footbridge at Shipley Gate. BR blue celebrity No. 37308 passes on the Up main with 7M18 09.55 Doncaster Decoy Yard–Toton Yard. Trees prevent the shot on the main now, and a signalling relay room blocks the view of the slow too. (19 March 2004)

No. 40009 passes Shipley Gate with the Class 40 Preservation Society's Cambrian Coast Express railtour, 1Z10 Manchester Victoria–Aberystwyth. (22 July 1984; courtesy of M. Slater)

Just north of the footbridge by a couple of hundred yards is a clearing in the trees. From here we see No. 66421 *Gresty Bridge TMD* passing Shipley Gate with a new service on the Erewash that commenced in the latter part of 2019, 4M51 06.38 Tees Dock–Daventry Tesco containers. Photo taken with the camera mounted on a pole. (3 December 2019)

No. 56060 passes Shipley Gate with 6M18 10.00 Doncaster Decoy Yard–Toton Yard conveying Network Rail Falcon open wagons and autoballasters. (2 March 2004)

Looking south from the same spot, No. 56048, in red stripe Railfreight livery, heads north along the Down goods line with 6D08 14.23 Witton–Whitwell Quarry stone empties. (26 June 1991; courtesy of D. Peachey)

A real mixed freight is seen heading north at Langley, with No. 37378 powering and No. 08517 hitching a ride on 8E71 Bescot Yard–Healey Mills Yard. (27 May 1988; courtesy of D. Peachey)

A really unusual working took place on the Erewash on this day. Class 50s D449, D444 and D431 were all moving light locos from the Severn Valley Railway to Barrow Hill, but at Toton they collected three SPA wagons and ran from there as 6Z60 13.28 Toton Yard–Barrow Hill, seen passing Lee Lane, Langley. (1 November 2001)

No. 56106 thrashes past Lee Lane footbridge at Langley, working 6E97 15.55 Corby steelworks–Aldwarke loaded scrap. (12 October 2002)

No. 37248 *Midland Railway Centre* and No. 37707 pass Lee lane, Langley, with 7B18 14.14 Ambergate Junction–Toton Yard engineering train conveying forty-five vacuum-braked MGV clam wagons. (7 April 2002)

Class 50 Fund-owned, but leased by GBRf, No. 50007 (masquerading as No. 50014 *Warspite*) leads stored ex-EMR-operated power cars Nos 43061 and 43075, with No. 50049 *Defiance* on the rear, as 0Z88 13:15 Tyne Yard–Chaddesden Yard seen passing through Langley Mill station. (26 March 2020; courtesy of I. Bowler)

No. 37801 sits in the Up platform at Langley Mill with 6B11 06.00 Stoneyford–Toton Yard possession train, though as the time I took the photo was around 10:00, the train was somewhat late. (4 June 2000)

No. 56049 rolls out of Langley Mill Yard with an MGR for Ratcliffe PS, which would have been brought down to the yard from Moorgreen colliery by one of their own industrial locos, which included three former BR Class 10s. (20 November 1978; courtesy of D. Peachey)

Moving on seven years and the footbridge has been renewed, and so has the traction, with No. 58009 passing on the Up goods line with another load of coal for Ratcliffe PS. The yard has also been abandoned after the closure of Moor Green Colliery. (1 November 1985; courtesy of D. Peachey)

Next we observe further changes, though it is thirty-four years since the No. 58009 photo was taken. No. 66617 passes Langley Mill with 6G65 09.19 Earles Sidings–Walsall cement. The local collieries, along with Langley Mill Yard, are now all but memories. (30 September 2019)

Just north of Langley Mill is Aldercar, where we see Nos 58016 and 58030 double heading a southbound MGR for Ratcliffe. (6 August 1992; courtesy of D. Peachey)

Looking south from the bridge at Aldercar, RES-liveried No. 47783 *Saint Peter* takes a charter north under heavy skies. (6 April 2001; courtesy of D. Peachey)

Viewed from the A610 bypass bridge, No. 37695 stands in an engineer's possession on the Up main at Stoneyford while the old ballast removed from the Down main formation is loaded to its train. (4 June 2000)

Performing a shunt at Stoneyford ground frame, No. 58043 sets back into the sidings with what is likely to be a loaded train bound for the Avenue coking plant from a Mansfield area colliery, which, which often used to use this location to run round rather than work through to Toton. In 2001 an open-cast disposal point known as Forge and Monument was opened here but, along with the majority of the rest of this country's coal industry, has long since disappeared. (12 April 1989; courtesy of D. Peachey)

Loco-hauled passenger work on the Erewash employs departmental grey-liveried No. 31462 with four NSE Mk 11s as they pass Stoneyford with the 09.57 Sheffield–Skegness. (7 September 1991; courtesy of D. Peachey)

The footbridge at Codnor Park, known locally as 'Monkey Bridge', is the location we see No. 37676 passing with an Earles sidings–Beeston cement train on the Up goods line. The departure line out of Codnor Park sidings can be glimpsed on the right. (6 July 1992; courtesy of D. Peachey)

Slightly further north sees the classic sweeping view at Codnor Park as No. 56126 glides through with another Ratcliffe PS-bound MGR train. (27 February 1986; courtesy of B. Dean)

On this day the photographer was somewhat bemused to see 6T15 10.14 Toton Yard–Doe Hill approach with the train loco No. 58030 silent and dead. However, bringing up the rear were the rescue party with No. 47784 *Condover Hall*, Nos 31271, 45133, 45041 *Royal Tank Regiment* and No. 58016 providing the traction to both the MGR and the convoy. No. 58016 uncoupled from the convoy just around the curve at Ironville to leave the Class 47 to push the convoy onto the preserved line, with the Class 58 pushing the MGR to its destination (also see page 90). (14 October 1996; courtesy of D. Peachey)

No. 37717 *Berwick Middle School Railsafe Trophy Winners 1998* sits shut down in an engineering possession at Codnor Park Junction, having arrived as 6B05 22.30 ex-Toton Yard. (20 August 2000)

One of the classic trains of the Erewash, the Tubeliner is seen at Codnor Park behind Thornaby's No. 37095 *British Steel Teeside* and No. 37062 *British Steel Corby* as 6M47 08.34 Lackenby Yard–Corby steelworks. (4 October 1985; courtesy of B. Dean)

A brief sojourn onto the Midland Railway branch, which is connected to the main line at Ironville. Deltic No. 55015 *Tulyar* top and tailing with No. 31162 approaching Swanwick Junction on the 13.00 Riddings–Butterley during a spring diesel gala. (18 March 1995)

Being main line connected has seen visiting locos provided for galas such as DRS-operated No. 20314 working with D5580 approaching Swanwick Junction with the 15.02 Riddings–Hammersmith. Occasional freight traffic also operated to and from the Butterley Engineering Company prior to them falling into administration in 2009. (27 March 1999)

No. 60053 *Nordic Terminal* stands at Ironville Junction within a possession with 6B03 23.05 Toton Yard–Codnor Park Junction. (13 June 2007; courtesy of V. Hardy)

During another engineering possession No. 37154 is seen at Pye Bridge Junction with 6B13 05.45 Trowell–Chaddesden Yard, waiting to exit the possession and head north to run round and return to Toton. (13 June 1999)

Heading south at Pye Bridge is No. 56081 with more coal for Ratcliffe PS, passing a smart building that was in use by the local permanent way team. (26 April 1989; courtesy of D. Peachey)

Nos 20210 and 20151 head north with empty MGR wagons heading to Sutton Colliery. Visible above the trees is the top of the Jessop monument, erected in 1854 as a memory to William Jessop Jnr, an active partner in the local Butterley company. (8 May 1989; courtesy of D. Peachey)

GBRf-operated No. 66766 approaches Ironville Junction working 7M18 07.21 Doncaster Up Decoy Yard–Toton Yard network infrastructure working, which on this day consisted of a long welded rail delivery train. The route diverging to the right is the branch to Kirkby in Ashfield via Pinxton. (25 February 2020)

We now take a quick visit to see a couple of locations on the Pinxton branch. Here we see No. 60031 passing Pinxton signal box with 6T97 07.31 Toton Yard–Welbeck Colliery empty MGR – note the dint at the bottom of the cab behind the left buffer. Upon closure of the signal box, when the line was encompassed in the Erewash resignalling in August 2007, it was saved and now resides at Barrow Hill. (11 October 2001)

The classic view on this route is from the M1 embankment at Pinxton. Here No. 47727 is seen from the eastern side on the rear of 5Q11 10.43 Derby Litchurch Lane–Worksop Yard, with the formation being led by No. 47749. The train is conveying new unit No. 720510 for storage pending its acceptance by Greater Anglia. The formation of the former Bentinck colliery branch can be seen next to No. 47727.

Back on the Erewash proper and No. 60031 *ABP Connect* is seen again, this time at Birchwood Lane, Somercotes, working 6M55 Lindsey OR–Rectory Junction loaded oil. Note the loco still has the dint in the cab between the left buffer and coupling, even after being repainted. (5 February 2009; courtesy of V. Hardy)

Class 50s No. 50031 *Hood* and No 50049 *Defiance* pass Birchwood Lane, Somercotes, with 5Z56 11.42 York Holgate sidings–Old Oak Common charter ECS. This is yet another location since by compromised by tree growth. (23 September 2002; courtesy of M. Slater)

Just out of view in the previous Class 50 shot is the footbridge just south of Alfreton tunnel, where we see No. 58024 exiting with more 'Black Gold' for Ratcliffe PS. Tree growth here now prevents a decent angle being obtained and also causes shadow problems. (11 June 1986; courtesy of B. Dean)

Approaching the north end of Alfreton tunnel are Nos 20032 and 20039 working 1E07 07.10 Sheffield–Skegness. The locos would be working hard, having just restarted away from the station stop at Alfreton. (14 June 1986; courtesy of B. Dean)

Nos 20188 and 20101 are seen between Alfreton tunnel and the station with a Toton Yard–Beighton Yard engineers' train. This view is still possible from the road bridge, but the background is now hidden by lineside trees. (28 May 1986; courtesy of B. Dean)

In what looks like lucky light, Peak No. 45134 restarts from the Alfreton & Mansfield Parkway stop with 1M84 17.10 Sheffield–Nottingham. This view has long been lost to vegetation growth. (9 April 1986; courtesy of B. Dean)

Another photographer captures No. 56088 as it screams through Alfreton station with yet another MGR on the Erewash Valley Line. A more head-on shot is still available here, but this angle is again compromised by vegetation. (26 March 1986; courtesy of B. Dean)

North of Alfreton station, EWS-liveried No. 66122 is seen at Blackwell South Junction, Westhouses, with 4Z52 06.35 Tees Dock–Daventry Tesco containers. This service is a DRS working and the loco has been hired by them, along with several other Class 66s from DB Cargo, to allow DRS to phase out some of their older traction types. Taken with a camera pole. (27 February 2020)

After being cruelly thwarted by a rogue cloud at Burton upon Trent, I chased Nos 57009 and 57008 *Telford International Railfreight Terminal June – 2009* working 4E38 Ditton–Tees Yard to Westhouses, where I was luckier with the light. (9 August 2012)

No. 56062 is seen among another two classmates and a pair of Class 20s between duties on Westhouses shed, a location that disappeared before I was out and about with camera equipment. (18 November 1983; courtesy of C. Smith)

A typical view of Westhouses with Class 20s abounding; Nos 20070 and 20134 are closest to the camera. The third loco behind No. 20134 appears to be a green-liveried, TOPS-numbered example. (12 July 1975; P. Robertson Collection)

Nos 31553 and 31558 *Nene Valley Railway* run along the Blackwell loop line at Westhouses, likely to allow a faster passenger service to precede them through to Alfreton. The train is conveying long welded rails on a slinger train, thought to be a Castleton to Toton working. Tibshelf sidings are by this time out of use, with rust and nature starting to take hold. (*c.* 1994; courtesy of S. Sterland)

During an afternoon shift at work No. 66953 became a failure at Chesterfield station and required assistance. With Freightliner's nearest loco being at Earles, this allowed me to purloin a loco to clear the line in emergency. A call to Serco Railtest provided No. 37667 and a driver from Derby RTC to run as 1Z99 to assist the train forward to Blackwell loop. Here No. 37667 is seen dragging No. 66953 and 6M01 11.19 Tinsley–Bardon Hill at Westhouses. The site of Tibshelf sidings has now been lost to a sea of vegetation. (Courtesy of J. Cross)

DRS-operated Nos 47501 and 47712 top and tail the Cargo-D blue and grey charter set north through Westhouses, running as 1Z93 06.00 Leicester to Carlisle. (10 July 2010; courtesy of M. Slater)

No. 70016 passes Doe Hill Country Park with 6G65 09.19 Earles Sidings–Walsall loaded cement. Taken with a camera pole. The country park is on the site of the former Doe Hill open-cast mine, the site being returned to nature by the Banks mining company upon closure of the site. (16 March 2020)

No. 56018, in sparkling condition, passes Doe Hill with 7M63 08.19 Doncaster Wood Yard–Mountsorrel ballast empties. (28 June 2000; courtesy of S. Sterland)

From the same bridge, but now on the evening side for the light, No. 58011 *Worksop Depot* is seen at Doe Hill working an Oxcroft–Ratcliffe PS MGR. (26 June 1991; courtesy of S. Sterland)

No. 37219 heads north along the Up and Down Blackwell loop at Doe Hill, working 6M21 09.11 Toton Yard–Castleton empty CWR train. This view of the loop line is now blocked by vegetation, but the main lines are still okay. (12 June 1997; courtesy of S. Sterland)

No. 58030 stands on the stop block at Doe Hill Disposal Point while its train, 6T15 10.14 from Toton, is loaded with coal for Ratcliffe Power Station. It was very unusual to see a loco at the blocks as they always ran round and backed in, but on this day (as seen on page 75) No. 58030 failed with a loss of oil, evidenced on the frame and bogie at No. 1 end. It was pushed into the siding by No. 58016, having been uncoupled from its convoy of preserved locos at Ironville, which it had been hauling to Butterley MRC. (14 October 1996; courtesy of D. Peachey)

DRS-operated No. 66431 rounds the curve at Danesmoor with 6E42 07.15 Stud Farm Quarry–Doncaster Decoy Yard bulk ballast working, bringing stone to Network Rail's virtual quarry storage location for use in engineering renewals. (6 March 2020)

No. 66126, a DB cargo loco on long-term hire to DRS, is seen from Pilsley Road bridge, Danesmoor, with 4Z52 06.35 South Bank Tees Dock–Daventry Tesco intermodal service. This service has since been retimed to run south overnight. (6 March 2020)

Taken from a spot near the back of the train in the previous picture, No. 60044 is literally sparkling in ex-works condition as its curves through Danesmoor with 6M23 12.57 Doncaster Up Decoy–Mountsorrel ballast empties. This location is now behind industrial buildings and access may be difficult. (14 November 2013)

Looking the opposite way on the former wasteland at Danesmoor, No. 66623 *Bill Bolsover* in its unique Bardon blue livery heads north with West Thurrock to Tunstead cement empties. (16 May 2016; courtesy of S. Sterland)

Taken from Market Street bridge, Coney Green, No. 44007 waits at the signal for a path to return to Toton from Tinsley as super clean No. 45019 works north on an empty steel working. The slow lines here were removed several years ago and only an Up and Down main remain. (*c.* July 1980; courtesy of S. Sterland)

No. 70014 sweeps around the curve at Coney Green working 6M73 10.52 Doncaster Up Decoy Yard–Toton Yard network infrastructure train, conveying concrete sleepers for use on the High Output Track Renewal System Train (TRS), which was based at Toton at the time. Class 70s were the regular power for this service in the early part of 2020, but they are now rarely seen on this service. (15 January 2020)

Viewed from the footbridge just north of Market Street bridge, DCR No. 56311 works a 6Z34 15.00 Chaddesden Yard–Shipley empty scrap train. (28 June 2012; courtesy of S. Bennett)

No. 66619 *Derek W. Johnson MBE* powers around the curve from Clay Cross to Coney Green with 6L89 11.48 Tunstead–Thorney Mill loaded stone. Due to operating restrictions at Thorney Mill this train is top and tailed on this day by No. 66591. (26 February 2020)

No. 47112 sweeps around from Coney Green to Clay Cross with 6E22 Spondon–Tinsley Speedlink. You guessed it, this view is long lost to tree growth. (16 April 1991; courtesy of C. Brogdale)

Coming off the Erewash and across the point work at Clay Cross South Junction is NSE-liveried No. 47573 *The London Evening Standard*, which was a pleasant surprise for the photographer, working 6E22 Spondon–Tinsley Speedlink. The opposite cants on the point work here were a particularly troublesome issue. (3 July 1981; P. Robertson collection)

No. 66560 approaches Clay Cross divergence on the Up Erewash line with 4O95 12.12 Leeds FLT–Southampton MCT. When the area was resignalled and remodelled, the point work of the junction was relocated to Tupton, beyond the back of the train, and renamed Clay Cross North Junction. The routes merely diverge now on the south side of this road bridge with no physical connection. (26 February 2020)

With the relocation of the junction between the Erewash Valley and the route to/from Derby to Tupton, now known as Clay Cross North Junction, the Erewash line was effectively extended by around half a mile. Here No. 46027 is seen approaching the location of where the new junction would be sited with a Loughborough–Beighton loaded ballast train with a rake of smartly turned-out Seacow hoppers. (3 July 1981; courtesy of P. Robertson collection)

Bibliography

Rhodes, Michael, *From Gridiron to Grassland: The Rise and Fall of Britain's Railway Marshalling Yards* (Lavenham: Platform 5 Publishing, 2016)

Copeland, David, *Toton Yards and the Erewash Valley: A Brief Railway History* (Peterborough: EMAP, 1998)